A SUPER HERO MEETS HIS ANGELS

Written By, Susan Cuccia
Illustrated By, Janie McMahan

About The Author

Susan Cuccia A.K.A SusanaBaNana lives in Southern California with her husband, Frank. They have been married fifty-six years. She has two grown children and five grandchildren. Susan's passion and love for children and the elderly led her to clown college where she learned to entertain and bring joy and laughter to others.

Now she is the author of two books. Walk a Mile in My Paws and Switch and A Superhero Meets His Angels. Soon to be released, A Superhero his Angel and The Haunted Bell Tower!

You can learn more about Susan at

www.susancuccia.com

Dedication

I dedicate this book to the war torn children of Ukraine. Who have to face fear every day and to all children who have monsters under their bed.

To my grandchildren who inspire me and to my grandson, Jonah, who is in the book.

Thank you to my beautiful granddaughter, Alyssa, who sings the lullaby and for creating my website.

You can hear Alyssa sing on my website and learn the words and tune. The music will also be posted at
www.susancuccia.com

Psalms 91:10-11

About The Illustrator

Janie McMahan has been painting and drawing as a hobby since childhood.

She is now retired from a career in high-tech and is painting full-time. She has collected children's books over the years and hoped one day to write and illustrate a children's book of her own.

When Susan Cuccia, a dear family friend, asked Janie if she would be interested in illustrating her story about a little Boy named Jonah and his Angels - she jumped at the chance!

In a charming little town called Upland, is a house with an orange door like a pumpkin.

In the front yard is a bicycle track and

a trampoline that sits in the back.

An adventurous and courageous boy named Jonah
lives in the house.

He runs and he plays and never tires out.

There's a very tall pine tree in the front yard,
Jonah is sure if he could climb to the top,
he could swing from the stars.

So every day, he climbs the knotted rope that
hangs from the tree, but for all his hard work,
all he gets are scraped knees.

He's the fearless flyer when riding his bike,
over the bumps he flies out of sight.

Back flips, front flips on the trampoline,
acrobats and cartwheels on the balance beam.

One day, Jonah put on his superhero cape, he flexed his muscles and felt very brave.

He pretended to fly around the yard yelling, "Look mom, I'm the Superhero guard."

His little dog Marsha followed in close pursuit, until she decided to stop and take a poop.

All of a sudden, Jonah heard a shrill cry.

He stopped and stared into a coyote's vicious eyes.

The coyote had Marsha in his hungry mouth.

Superhero Jonah screamed and gave a threatening shout.

The coyote just stood there unafraid.

His eyes dared Jonah, *"Let's see if you are really brave!"*

Little does the coyote know, Jonah is brave as well as smart.

He picked up some rocks and gets a bullseye shot!

He hit the coyote square in the head.

The coyote dropped Marsha and ran to his den!

But like Superman with kryptonite, there are monsters that cause Jonah's hair to stand straight up with fright.

So when Momma says "It's time for bed,"
Jonah fears the monsters that play in his head.

Jonah says, "I'm not tired, I don't want to go to bed. Let me stay up and play instead."

He cries and stomps his feet, "Please mommy don't make me go to sleep."

Momma says, "What's really troubling you?" Jonah replies, "I'm scared when you leave the room and I'm alone in the dark, I'm not a courageous Superhero anymore. My courage seems to melt away,

I'm a scared-y-cat, I'm a coward and I'm afraid.
I hear strange noises and I can't fall asleep, I fear a footless monster who wants to steal my feet."

Momma says, "Let's take a peak under the bed."
"No footless monster there," she says.

Then they look in the closet and every corner of the room. They check the window and all they see is the moon.

"The footless monster is your imagination,
something of your own creation.

His name is Fear, and we can shoo him away.
We all have the power when we pray.

Remember when you rescued Marsha from the coyote
- how did you feel?"

"I was scared, I was so afraid, but when I heard
Marsha cry, I knew she had to be saved."

"Well, you see, Jonah, having courage doesn't mean
the absence of fear. Courage is the ability to do what
you are afraid of in spite of your fear."

Momma says, "I'll sing you a lullaby to relax you and put you to sleep, so you don't have to be afraid when I leave."

"God's Angels are here and will continue to sing. God sent them to protect you and they will never leave."

Momma sings softly the lullaby.
Jonah drifts off to sleep but still whimpers and cries.

The Angels begin to sing,
the crying stops and Jonah dreams.

He hears the Angels sing their song,
Momma thinks she hears Jonah humming along.

The Lullaby

The Angels are singing a lullaby,
dont't you cry, sweet child of mine.
The Angels are singing a lullaby

They whisper God's secrets in your little ear,
Jonah dearest Jonah the Angels are near.

To guard and protect you all day and all night,
so there's no need to fear or cry
everything's all right.

Can you feel the cool breeze from the Angels wings?
Can you feel their tender kiss on your soft cheek?

Can you feel their gentle hands as they rock you to sleep?
Are you dreaming of the Angels while you sleep?

Dream dream dreaming of the Angels.
Skipping on a rainbow
flying from star to star.
Dancing in the light God's loving light
Now all his fears are gone
cause he can hear the Angels,
Hear the Angels
Hear the Angels song!

America is praying for the children
of Ukraine.